Original title:

Dancing Companionship

Author: Mirell Mesipuu

ISBN HARDBACK: 978-1-80560-256-9

ISBN PAPERBACK: 978-1-80560-721-2

Harmony's Embrace

In the dawn, the soft light glows,
Nature whispers, the river flows.
Birds take flight in the open sky,
Together singing, as time slips by.

Leaves dance gently on the breeze,
Each moment's gift, a simple tease.
Flowers bloom, colors bright,
A canvas painted in pure delight.

Mountains stand with tranquil grace,
Embracing all in a warm embrace.
Waves crash softly on the shore,
Nature's rhythm, forevermore.

Hearts unite in the golden hour,
Shared laughter scents the fragrant flower.
Hands entwined, we find our way,
In harmony's grace, we long to stay.

Under the stars, dreams take flight,
A tapestry woven in the night.
Together we rise, never apart,
In harmony's embrace, love fills the heart.

Whispers of the Floor

Footsteps whisper softly here,
Echoes of the day so near.
Secrets held beneath the wood,
Stories shared where silence stood.

Every creak tells tales of old,
Moments captured, memories bold.
Fading light through dusty seams,
Life is woven through our dreams.

In the corners, shadows play,
Dancing lightly, drift away.
Beneath the surface, hearts ignite,
Whispers fade into the night.

Listen close, the floor will speak,
In every hush, the strong and weak.
Each mark and scratch, a voice in time,
Tales of sorrow, joy, and rhyme.

Two Hearts in Tandem

In the quiet, two hearts beat,
Rhythms echoing, love's sweet heat.
Side by side, through thick and thin,
Together always, where we begin.

Paths entwined in life's embrace,
Finding solace in each space.
With every laugh, with every tear,
Two souls dance, drawing near.

Through storms and sun, we swiftly glide,
In tandem, we face the rising tide.
Whispers soft, promises bold,
Love's warm touch, a story told.

Navigating life's wild turns,
In each other, the fire burns.
Two hearts twined, forever true,
In this world, just me and you.

Unraveled in the Spin

Threads of time, they twist and twine,
Life's great tapestry, so divine.
In each circle, moments blend,
Past and present, a seamless mend.

Spinning slowly, shadows dance,
In the chaos, we find a chance.
Unravel tales from deep within,
As we twirl, let love begin.

Colors fade, then come alive,
In the spin, our spirits thrive.
What was lost will find its way,
Through the night, into the day.

Weaving dreams, our fates align,
In this rhythm, our hearts combine.
Embrace the process, trust the thread,
In every turn, our souls are fed.

Dance of the Twin Stars

In the sky, two sparks ignite,
Twinkling softly, pure delight.
Together they spin, a cosmic tune,
Dancing nightly, 'neath the moon.

Gravity pulls, yet they embrace,
Each rotation, a waltzing grace.
Lightyears apart, but close at heart,
Twin flames of creation, never apart.

In the silence, they share their dreams,
Whispers echo in starlit beams.
Through the ages, their bond will flow,
A dance eternal, a radiant glow.

Guided by love, they forge the way,
Lighting paths where shadows play.
Twin stars blazing, bright and free,
A celestial dance, just you and me.

Rhythms of Togetherness

In the dance of shared hearts,
We find the beat that plays,
Every step a gentle spark,
Lighting up our ways.

Hands entwined, we journey forth,
Through valleys deep and wide,
With laughter echoing around,
In joy, we do abide.

Silent whispers in the night,
A bond that feels so right,
Like stars that softly glow,
Together, we ignite.

Seasons change, yet we remain,
In cycles of embrace,
The rhythms of our hearts,
Forever interlaced.

With every heartbeat's thrum,
Our symphony does play,
In the tides of life we trust,
Together, come what may.

Chasing Shadows in the Moonlight

Beneath the silvery glow,
We wander hand in hand,
Chasing shadows lightly,
Across the dreamer's land.

Whispers in the cool night breeze,
Guide us down the path,
Each step a gentle promise,
In love's warm aftermath.

The moonlight paints our faces,
With a shimmer soft and bright,
In the calm of midnight whispers,
We find our hearts alight.

Stars above, they watch us,
As we dance in time's embrace,
Two souls entwined forever,
In this cherished space.

In shadows, we find secrets,
Hidden in the night,
Together we are stronger,
As we step towards the light.

United in Motion

Together we will rise,
With hearts beating as one,
Through the storms, we will soar,
Facing battles won.

Every hurdle that we meet,
Shall be a chance to grow,
In the pulse of shared courage,
Our spirits overflow.

With synchronized footsteps,
We march to the same tune,
In a world that spins with chaos,
We are the calm and moon.

Through valleys and through peaks,
Our bond will not fade,
United we stand tall,
In the plans we have made.

As the shadows may linger,
We will light the way,
Hand in hand, forever strong,
In motion, we shall stay.

Footsteps on the Horizon

With each step on the sand,
We carve our dreams anew,
The horizon calls our names,
In the morning dew.

Golden rays kiss the earth,
While waves sing to the shore,
In every grain of time,
We will dance and soar.

The footprints left behind,
Tell stories of our past,
As we stride toward the sun,
In hopes that forever lasts.

Together we chase the dawn,
With hearts so wild and free,
Each moment is a treasure,
In this harmony.

On the edge of what may come,
We pursue with gentle grace,
Footsteps on the horizon,
Together, we embrace.

Glimmering Moments

In twilight's gentle glow,
Memories softly sway,
Flickers of light appear,
Whispering what they say.

Stars dance in the sky,
As dreams begin to spin,
Each spark a fleeting joy,
Where love's stories begin.

Breezes carry laughter,
Through branches swaying high,
Nature's sweet caress calls,
Inviting us to fly.

Time weaves a bright thread,
Binding moments so dear,
In the fabric of life,
Glimmers that we hold near.

Embrace the now, the bright,
Each second, pure delight,
For every glimmer seen,
Is a heart's soft respite.

Rhythm of the Cosmos

In the stillness of night,
Stars hum a silent tune,
Galaxies swirl and spin,
Cradled by silver moon.

A heartbeat echoing,
Through the infinite space,
Cosmic whispers beckon,
To this vast, endless place.

The planets softly dance,
In orbits so divine,
Each twirl a perfect step,
In the grand design.

Frequency of stardust,
In harmony they play,
Threads of time and wonders,
In the night's soft sway.

Feel the pulse of the night,
In every breath you take,
For within this rhythm,
Life's beauty will awake.

Chimes of Connection

Bells ring in the distance,
Echoes of hearts aligned,
Melodies that linger,
In body, soul, and mind.

With each gentle chime heard,
Barriers fade away,
In the warmth of the sound,
Connection finds its way.

Voices blend in the air,
A chorus born of trust,
Hand in hand we'll wander,
In harmony, we must.

Moments shared in silence,
Speak louder than a word,
In the tapestry of life,
Each thread brightly stirred.

Together, we'll keep ringing,
The chimes that we create,
For in each lovely note,
Lies a bond that won't abate.

Lyric of the Heart

In the stillness of dawn,
A song begins to rise,
Whispers fill the air,
Painting blue in the skies.

Each note a sweet promise,
Of love that knows no end,
In the depth of silence,
A symphony we send.

Strings weave through the moments,
Creating soft embrace,
The music of our lives,
In every shared space.

Feel the pulse of the beat,
In time, we dance as one,
With each lyric spoken,
New journeys have begun.

Let your heart keep singing,
To the rhythm of your soul,
For the lyric of the heart,
Is what makes us whole.

A Tapestry of Motion

In the weave of the winding road,
Life spins in threads, a vibrant code.
Colors blend, as moments flow,
Every twist reveals what we don't know.

Echoes of laughter fill the air,
Footsteps follow, unaware.
Time unfolds in gentle waves,
Stories linger in the paths it paves.

A dance of dreams beneath the sky,
Chasing clouds as they drift by.
Whispers linger in the breeze,
Reminding us to move with ease.

The rhythm of each beating heart,
Guiding journeys from the start.
With every pulse, we leave a mark,
Lighting up the dark with sparks.

Together we spin, a living art,
Each moment cherished, each a part.
In the tapestry, we find our place,
Embracing life's unending grace.

The Art of Connection

In a world adorned with silent ties,
Hearts whisper truths beneath the skies.
Fingers touch, and eyes intine,
In this dance, our souls align.

Words unspoken create a bond,
A gentle tug, a tethered respond.
In shared glances, we find our thread,
With every word left unsaid.

Together we weave a fragile lace,
Tangled pathways, a sacred space.
Minds embrace in the fleeting light,
Crafting dreams that take to flight.

Moments linger in tender caress,
Each heartbeat sings, a soft confess.
Through time and trials, we grow strong,
In the art of connection, we belong.

A melody sung in the quiet night,
Bringing comfort, warmth, and light.
Across the distance, love will bloom,
In the spaces where hearts find room.

Boundless Beats of Affection

Beneath the stars, our pulses rise,
In every glance, a sweet surprise.
Two hearts drumming rhythmic ties,
In boundless beats, our spirit flies.

Laughter echoes, a joyous sound,
In simple moments, love is found.
Dancing shadows on the ground,
In each heartbeat, we are bound.

Through fleeting days, we hold on tight,
In whispered dreams, we share the night.
Every hug, a sacred flow,
In boundless beats, together we grow.

Softened touches, a gentle sway,
Carving memories that softly play.
In every smile, our worlds align,
With boundless affection, hearts entwine.

As seasons change, we stand as one,
Chasing sunsets, sharing the sun.
Love's rhythm guides us, bold and true,
In boundless beats, I find you too.

When Shadows Dance Side by Side

In the twilight where whispers blend,
Shadows stretch, as daylight bends.
Figures move, a silent show,
When shadows dance, their secrets flow.

In the moonlight's gentle embrace,
We trace memories, a soft space.
Flickers of light, a shared delight,
When shadows sway in the night.

Echoes of laughter, a soft refrain,
In mirrored steps, we share the gain.
Footprints linger along the tide,
As day turns dark, we cannot hide.

Together we weave stories old,
In every shadow, a truth told.
In silent sways, our hearts confide,
When shadows dance, love won't divide.

Through the canvas of night, we'll glide,
In the magic where moments abide.
In shadows' waltz, we find our way,
Forevermore, where we shall stay.

Unfolding Journeys

Paths diverge beneath the sky,
Footsteps echo, moments fly.
With each turn, a story grows,
In the heart, adventure flows.

Mountains rise, the rivers bend,
Winds of change, they never end.
Stars above, they light the way,
Guiding dreams where shadows play.

In the stillness, whispers call,
A gentle push, we feel so small.
With every step, the search is real,
The world awaits, and wounds can heal.

Bridges built on trust and grace,
In the dance, we find our place.
Hand in hand, we traverse the night,
Unfolding journeys, hearts in flight.

Spellbound in Step

With every footfall, magic sways,
In rhythm, we find our ways.
A spell that binds the heart and soul,
As we dance towards the goal.

Leaves caress as breezes hum,
In this moment, we are one.
With laughter swirling in the air,
We embrace the love we share.

Colors clash in vibrant cheer,
As twilight whispers, night draws near.
In shadows cast, our spirits rise,
Spellbound beneath the painted skies.

Each heartbeat marks the time we take,
Magic brewed in each sweet shake.
In woven steps, we feel entwined,
A dance of fate we leave behind.

A Symphony of Solitude and Together

Silent notes in stillness play,
A melody that finds its way.
In shadows where we often roam,
Each echo brings us closer home.

Harmony in every breath,
Life entwined with love and death.
To be alone yet seek the light,
A symphony that feels so right.

Voices mingle in the void,
Dreams are tangled, yet enjoyed.
In whispers soft as summer rain,
Together still, through joy and pain.

In silence, we find the thread,
A tapestry in hues of red.
The heartful tune of souls that blend,
In solitude, we seek a friend.

Weaving Through Shadows

In a tapestry spun with care,
Threads of darkness, light to share.
Weaving through the afterglow,
Finding strength in what we know.

Echoes dance where shadows play,
Illuminated by the fray.
Whispers soft, they guide the way,
Through tangled paths, we choose to stay.

Layers deep, each story told,
In the shadows, hearts turn bold.
We cast our fears into the night,
In weaving whispers, find our light.

With intertwined dreams, we strive,
In every step, we come alive.
Among the darkness, hope's embrace,
Weaving through shadows, find our grace.

Footprints in the Sand

Upon the shore, where waves collide,
Footprints linger, then subside.
In mornings light, they slowly fade,
Memories lost, like dreams displayed.

The tide comes in, erasing past,
Yet in our hearts, those moments last.
Each step we took, each laugh we shared,
Marks of a journey, unprepared.

The sun sets low, in crimson hue,
The footprints tell of me and you.
With every wave that washes near,
Our love remains, forever clear.

In every grain, a tale we weave,
A fleeting touch, hard to believe.
Yet in the sand, our story stands,
A timeless bond, in golden strands.

With every storm, the sea will change,
But in my heart, you will remain.
These footprints on this sandy bed,
Are whispers of the life we led.

Echoing in the Silence

In quiet rooms, the shadows play,
Silent whispers drift away.
Thoughts a dance, unspoken words,
Echo softly, like distant birds.

In solitude, my heart can hear,
The echoes drawn from far and near.
Moments cherished, softly spoken,
In silence deep, no bonds are broken.

What once was loud, now fades to gray,
In stillness, where I long to stay.
Each memory a gentle sigh,
In silence strong, our dreams can fly.

Through empty halls, your laughter rings,
Resonating like the songs of springs.
Unseen threads connect our souls,
Echoing love, that makes us whole.

In nights profound, let echoes dwell,
In shades of calm, they weave a spell.
Though silence reigns, it speaks so true,
In every breath, I think of you.

The Flow Between Us

Like rivers running, wild and free,
There's a current, just you and me.
Through winding paths, we find our way,
In every moment, come what may.

The tides may turn, the winds may change,
Yet through it all, we stay in range.
A force unseen, it pulls us close,
In every heartbeat, it's you I chose.

Each drop of rain, a kiss from fate,
In every surge, the thrill we create.
Together drifting, side by side,
In this flow, we'll always bide.

Through every storm, we find reprieve,
In this river, we believe.
Let's ride the waves with hearts so bold,
In the flow, our love unfolds.

With every stroke, take hold of me,
In this dance of life, we are free.
The flow between us, pure and true,
In each embrace, I cherish you.

Jigsaw of Joy

Life's a puzzle with missing parts,
Each piece, a work of loving arts.
Together we build, a tapestry,
Of laughter, tears, and sweet harmony.

With every triumph, each little cheer,
We discover joy, when you are near.
Thankful for every colored hue,
In this jigsaw, I find you.

Though pieces scatter, lost at times,
We find our way through hills and climbs.
The picture forms as days unfold,
In every moment, our hearts behold.

Fragments of laughter, whispers sweet,
Every connection, a chance to meet.
In this dance, our spirits soar,
Completing the puzzle, forever more.

As we connect, the colors blend,
Creating a masterpiece, around the bend.
With each addition, our love will grow,
In this jigsaw of joy, I love you so.

Swaying Hearts

In the gentle breeze, we sway,
Whispers of love guide the way.
Hands entwined beneath the stars,
Time stands still, forgetting scars.

Soft melodies cradle our fears,
In your eyes, the world appears.
Each heartbeat echoes a tune,
Underneath the silver moon.

Our laughter dances with the night,
In this moment, all feels right.
With every sway, we draw near,
Lost in the magic, sincere.

As shadows blend, our dreams ignite,
Two swaying hearts take to flight.
In this embrace, we find our place,
Forever bound in love's grace.

The Waltz of Souls

Beneath the glow of twilight skies,
Two souls waltz, where magic lies.
With every step, a story flows,
In the dusk, their passion grows.

The rhythm swells as shadows play,
A dance of fate that won't decay.
In each twirl, they find the spark,
An eternal flame in the dark.

Their laughter rings, a sweet refrain,
A melody that soothes their pain.
They glide in circles, lost in trance,
In the wonder of their dance.

With every twirl, a promise made,
In this moment, doubts do fade.
Together in the night they find,
The waltz of souls, forever aligned.

In Step with Dreams

In the quiet hours of night,
Dreams take flight, hearts feel light.
Together we tread through the haze,
Chasing stars, lost in a maze.

With every step, hope takes form,
In the calm before the storm.
Through shadows deep, we march ahead,
With courage strong, no fear of dread.

In each heartbeat, a vision grows,
In step with dreams, our love flows.
Together we'll paint the skies bright,
With swirling colors, pure delight.

As dawn breaks, our dreams align,
Hand in hand, your heart is mine.
In the light, our path we'll weave,
In step with dreams, we believe.

Harmony in the Twilight

In twilight's glow, our spirits sing,
Harmony flows with gentle wing.
With whispers sweet, the night unfolds,
In its embrace, our love beholds.

Melodies dance on fading light,
In this realm, everything feels right,
Together we roam through the night,
Hand in hand, hearts shining bright.

The stars align, our journey starts,
Each note a pulse, in sync with hearts.
As shadows blend, we feel the peace,
In harmony's arms, we find release.

The world drifts away, just us two,
In twilight's song, forever true.
With every breath, and every sigh,
Harmony reigns as time slips by.

Choreographed Moments

In silence we convene, a gentle sway,
Each heartbeat moves, in soft ballet.
With eyes that speak, and hands that weave,
A dance unfolds, in a world we believe.

The music swells, a tender tune,
As shadows tango beneath the moon.
Every glance a step, every breath a turn,
In this rhythm of love, we eternally yearn.

Together we pirouette through time's embrace,
Each moment cherished, in this sacred space.
With laughter as notes, and whispers as grace,
We choreograph dreams, in a timeless race.

The world fades away, as we intertwine,
In the echo of hearts, our spirits align.
With every dip and lift, we rise anew,
Choreographed moments, just me and you.

Infinite Twirls

We spin like stars in an endless night,
Each twirl a dream, a burst of light.
Around and around, in joyous flight,
In the dance of life, we find our might.

With laughter painting colors in the air,
Each step we take, a love affair.
In dizzying patterns, so bold and rare,
We lose ourselves, without a care.

The ground beneath fades, as we rise high,
In this dance of freedom, we touch the sky.
With every turn, our spirits fly,
Infinite twirls, as the moments pass by.

Together we weave through the fabric of time,
In the rhythm of hearts, our souls will chime.
Every pulse a promise, every beat a rhyme,
Twisting in joy, so sublime.

Through swirling skies, we'll always roam,
In the infinite twirls, we find our home.

A Canvas of Distant Echoes

On canvas wide, memories collide,
Each brushstroke whispers, where shadows hide.
With hues of longing and shades of grace,
A tapestry woven, time can't erase.

Across the distances, soft echoes play,
In twilight's hush, they gently sway.
With every color, a tale unfolds,
Of love and loss, in whispers told.

The beauty of distance, a bittersweet song,
In every note, we find where we belong.
Lost in the echoes, we linger long,
A canvas of memories, forever strong.

In the gallery of time, our hearts reside,
Among painted skies, dreams undenied.
Each echo a heartbeat, as worlds collide,
In this art of living, where love abides.

Through time and space, we create and dream,
On this canvas vast, life's endless stream.

Starlight Sequences

Beneath the stars, we trace the night,
In sequences of starlight, pure and bright.
With constellations guiding our way,
We dance to the rhythm, where spirits play.

Each twinkle a promise, a wish set free,
In the vast expanse of infinity.
With cosmic breaths, our souls align,
In starlit whispers, like sacred wine.

We weave through darkness, hand in hand,
In the tapestry of galaxies, we stand.
With every heartbeat, another star shines,
In this celestial dance, our love entwines.

Lost in the magic of midnight's embrace,
We find ourselves in this timeless space.
Each star a memory, each memory a trace,
In the starlight sequences, we leave our grace.

Together we blaze, across the abyss,
In the dance of the cosmos, an infinite kiss.

Unbroken Circles

In timeless space we spin,
Bound by threads unseen,
Each moment brings us close,
A dance of silent dreams.

With laughter bright as dawn,
We trace our steps in light,
The echoes of our joy,
Resound through endless night.

Boundless hearts entwined,
The world fades all away,
In perfect harmony,
We find our truest play.

Through storms and quiet days,
Our bond will not grow weak,
In the circle of our love,
It's trust that we now seek.

Together we will roam,
In circles ever wide,
To know you is to live,
With you, I will abide.

The Dance of Familiar Souls

In shadows of the past,
We find our gentle grace,
With every whispered word,
We know this sacred space.

The memories we share,
They twirl like autumn leaves,
In this familiar waltz,
Our souls find what they need.

A rhythm soft and sweet,
The heartbeat of our trust,
In each other's presence,
We rise from all the dust.

The dance goes on and on,
With laughter as our guide,
In every step we take,
Our spirits gently glide.

Through seasons that may change,
We hold to what feels right,
In the dance of our hearts,
We shine with purest light.

Strung Together

Like beads upon a thread,
Our lives in patterned grace,
Each struggle, joy, and tear,
A story to embrace.

Through laughter and through pain,
We find a vibrant hue,
A tapestry of dreams,
Woven from me and you.

Each moment echoes loud,
In colors bold and bright,
Together we create,
A world forged in our light.

The threads may sometimes fray,
Yet still, we stitch anew,
In unity we stand,
Our hearts, forever true.

Strung together, we shine,
A necklace of our fears,
With every passing day,
We gather all our years.

Where Our Shadows Meet

In twilight's soft embrace,
We linger, side by side,
Where shadows weave their dance,
With secrets yet untied.

The world fades far away,
As whispering winds conspire,
To blend our tales as one,
In dusk's warm, tender fire.

With every heartbeat shared,
Time holds its breath in awe,
In this sacred pause,
We find what we're here for.

The sun dips low and sings,
As stars begin to glow,
In the space between us,
The mysteries unfold.

Together in the dark,
Our spirits find their light,
Where shadows meet and blend,
We rise into the night.

Synchronized Steps

Together we dance in perfect time,
Each step a whisper, each breath a rhyme.
Under the stars, we lose all fear,
In this moment, everything is clear.

Hearts beating fast, we glide and sway,
Lost in the music, we fade away.
Every turn brings us closer still,
This harmony sings, an unbroken thrill.

Side by side, we move as one,
The dawn is breaking, our night is done.
With every leap, our spirits rise,
In the ballet of life, we reach for the skies.

Footsteps echo in the gentle night,
Guided by moonbeams, we find our light.
Together we'll dance through every storm,
In the rhythm of love, we will transform.

As the world fades, it's just you and me,
In synchronized steps, we're wild and free.
Through valleys and peaks, a journey vast,
In this dance of life, forever we'll last.

The Language of Movement

Words unspoken, yet clearly defined,
In every gesture, our hearts entwined.
A tilt of the head, a soft glance shared,
In the dance of life, we're completely bared.

Fingers trace paths through the air we breathe,
Each motion a story, a tale to weave,
When bodies align, the world feels whole,
In this quiet ballet, we touch the soul.

Rhythms pulse deep, like a beating drum,
A dance of the senses, where all voices hum.
With every sway, we connect anew,
In this silent dialogue, our spirits flew.

Echoes of laughter, footsteps in sync,
In the dance of shadows, we pause to think.
Every twirl paints a picture profound,
In this language of movement, love knows no bound.

Together we shine, in the stillness we find,
The whispers of hearts, perfectly aligned.
Through fluid motions, we create and mend,
In this vivid connection, there's no end.

Intertwined Rhythms

In the spiral of time, we find our way,
With beats that echo both night and day.
Like rivers flowing, we merge and part,
In the symphony of life, you stole my heart.

Every heartbeat resonates in tune,
Under the gaze of the silver moon.
With dance as our guide, we leap and waltz,
In the fabric of movement, we spin our faults.

Hand in hand, we travel the floor,
In a swirl of colors, forevermore.
Our bodies speak what words cannot say,
In the collage of rhythm, we twine and sway.

Through highs and lows, together we dive,
In this universe, we come alive.
With each step forward, new pathways we trace,
In the echo of sound, there's a warm embrace.

With hearts entwined, we pulse as one,
In synchronized chaos, the dance has begun.
Together we flow, our destinies bind,
In this moment of magic, our souls unwind.

Conversations in the Breeze

Whispers of wind carry tales of old,
In the dance of the leaves, secrets unfold.
With each gentle gust, we share our dreams,
In the sweetness of nature, everything beams.

Under the boughs where shadows play,
Thoughts take flight in a carefree way.
Hands uplifted, we follow the breeze,
In the symphony of trees, we find our ease.

Soft rustlings speak in a language so rare,
In the hush of the forest, we drift without care.
Every sigh of the wind, a note so pure,
In this floating dialogue, we feel secure.

Colliding with laughter, the clouds drift high,
In the canvas of sky, our spirits can fly.
With every soft whisper, a story is spun,
In conversations with nature, our hearts are one.

So let the wind carry our tales far and wide,
In its gentle embrace, we shall abide.
Through rustling branches and whispers of trees,
In the dance of the breeze, our souls find ease.

The Grace of Together

In the quiet whispers of the night,
Hands entwined, we hold on tight.
Every moment feels like grace,
In your eyes, I find my place.

Through storms that might oppose our way,
Side by side, we choose to stay.
With laughter shared and hopes that gleam,
Together we create a dream.

Like rivers flowing, free and wise,
Our hearts connect, no need for disguise.
With every step, we boldly take,
The bond we share will never break.

In the garden where our visions bloom,
We nurture love, dispel the gloom.
With petals soft and roots that run,
Together, two become as one.

In twilight's glow, the day departs,
But in our union, light imparts.
With courage found in every tether,
We dance through life, the grace of together.

Delight in the Drift

As leaves float down in autumn's grace,
We find our joy in time and space.
With gentle breezes, we embrace,
The simple moments we can trace.

Like clouds that wander, soft and free,
We chase the whims of destiny,
With laughter bright, we lift our way,
In every drift, we find our play.

On sandy shores where waves retreat,
We dance with joy, our hearts compete.
With grains of time slipping through,
Delight is found in what we do.

In twilight's glow, as day takes flight,
We revel in the fading light.
With every second that we give,
Each drift becomes a way to live.

In dreams that guide us from above,
We wander on, a dance of love.
With open hearts, we choose to lift,
In every moment, delight in the drift.

Entwined Echoes

In the hushed corners of the night,
Echoes linger, soft and light.
Two voices blend in sweet refrain,
A harmony that breaks the chain.

Through valleys deep, our laughter flows,
In shadows cast, our courage grows.
With every heartbeat, memories call,
Entwined echoes, we shall not fall.

In whispered tales beneath the stars,
Together we heal, no more scars.
With every tear and every cheer,
Our echoes dance, forever near.

Across the miles, like threads of gold,
We weave our stories, brave and bold.
In every silence, love will swell,
Entwined echoes, where hearts dwell.

In twilight's embrace, our dreams collide,
With every step, we dance with pride.
In every note, our souls unite,
Together, we'll echo through the night.

The Softness of Our Stomp

As footsteps fall on morning dew,
We tread softly, just me and you.
With laughter light and whispers sweet,
Each moment shared makes life complete.

In meadows green, we leave our trace,
With gentle strides, we find our place.
Through fields of dreams, our spirits roam,
The softness of our stomp feels like home.

With echoes soft on forest trails,
Our hearts a rhythm, love prevails.
In every pause, in every leap,
The softness binds us, strong and deep.

As seasons change and time flows on,
We dance through challenges, never gone.
With each soft step, we create the time,
The softness of our stomp, a rhyme.

With evening's glow and starlit skies,
We trace the paths where comfort lies.
Together we walk, forever bold,
In the softness of our stomp, stories unfold.

Tides of Togetherness

The waves roll gently in and out,
We walk hand in hand, no doubt.
In the dance of the brimming tide,
Our hearts become the ocean's guide.

Sunset paints the sky with gold,
Memories we've cherished, bold.
With each rhythm, we find our place,
In this world of warm embrace.

Stars begin to twinkle bright,
Each one shares a secret light.
Our laughter echoes through the night,
In our hearts, the joy feels right.

Together we set sail anew,
With every moment, love feels true.
The tides may rush, or ebb away,
But together, we'll always stay.

The moon whispers a soothing song,
In this journey, we belong.
With the ocean as our friend,
Together, we will never end.

The Tango of Trust

In the embrace of twilight's hue,
Two souls dance in steps so true.
The rhythm beats, our hearts align,
In the trust where love can shine.

Footsteps whisper secrets known,
Guided by love, never alone.
With every turn, we find our way,
In this dance, we choose to stay.

Hands entwined, we face the night,
With every step, our spirits light.
Together we weave a tale so grand,
In the tango, we take a stand.

Moments twirl like autumn leaves,
In this trust, our heart believes.
With every glance, a promise made,
In the dance, our fears do fade.

As the music softens and slows,
In each other's arms, our love grows.
With every sway, we find release,
In the tango, our hearts find peace.

Lullaby of the Light

The dawn breaks soft with tinted grace,
A gentle glow upon your face.
With whispers of a brand new day,
The light sings in a sweet ballet.

Stars fade in the morning glow,
A lullaby that whispers low.
The sun awakens dreams held tight,
In golden beams, there's pure delight.

With every beam, a story's spun,
Of laughter shared and battles won.
In the warmth of the rising sun,
Our hearts rejoice, our journey's begun.

The shadows fall, retreating slow,
As light embraces what we know.
In the morning, love's tender sight,
Guides us through, a sweet respite.

Let the light be our gentle guide,
In its warmth, we can confide.
With open hearts, we take our flight,
To follow the lullaby of light.

Partners in the Night

Beneath the veil of twilight's grace,
We find our rhythm, a sacred space.
With whispered dreams and hearts aligned,
In this moment, our souls entwined.

The moon casts shadows, cool and bright,
As we wander through the night
Each step we take, a promise made,
In the darkness, love won't fade.

Stars above like diamonds gleam,
Reflecting all our hopes and dreams.
Together we paint the sky anew,
In every wish, it's me and you.

The night wraps us in soft delight,
As we dance beneath the stars' light.
With every laugh and every sigh,
Our love works wonders, soaring high.

As dawn approaches with its glow,
Our hearts still dance, moving slow.
In the stillness, we find our way,
Partners in the night, come what may.

Whispers of the Groove

In shadows deep, the echoes sway,
Soft rhythm calls, we dance and play.
A gentle hum, the night ignites,
Whispers of joy, through sweet delights.

The stars above, they twinkle bright,
Each step we take, feels so right.
Our hearts align, in perfect tune,
Together we shine, beneath the moon.

The bass, it thumps, a steady beat,
With every pulse, our spirits meet.
In every turn, in every glide,
The whispers bloom, we cannot hide.

A melody that fills the air,
With every note, we leave our care.
The groove goes deep, the night is long,
In this embrace, we find our song.

Joyful Reverberations

Laughter dances, vibrant sounds,
In joyful waves, our spirit bounds.
The echoes rise, they swell and grow,
In playful rhythm, we feel the flow.

Each smile shared, a spark ignites,
In every heart, a warmth, a light
Together here, our dreams take flight,
Joyful reverberations in the night.

The world around, a canvas bright,
We paint with cheer, hearts so light.
A chorus formed, in harmony,
The sweetest song, just you and me.

As moments pass, like fleeting streams,
We hold onto our cherished dreams.
With every beat, we dance along,
In joyful reverberations, we belong.

Spirited Encounters

Beneath the sun, where laughter calls,
We take a step, and then we fall.
Into embrace, where spirits blend,
In every glance, a new sweet friend.

The air is rich with stories spun,
In each encounter, two become one.
With open hearts, we share our tales,
In spirited moments, love prevails.

From strangers' eyes, the spark ignites,
We weave our paths, in dance of lights.
No words are needed, still we find,
A bond unspoken, intertwined.

In fleeting time, connections last,
In every meeting, shadows cast.
Through warming smiles, we feel the glow,
In spirited encounters, friendships flow.

Together We Glide

In gentle strides, the world we trace,
With every heartbeat, we find our place.
Through winding roads and trails unmade,
Together we glide, unafraid.

The sunlit path, it calls our name,
In every moment, we stake our claim.
With laughter shared, the journey's sweet,
Together in rhythm, we feel complete.

The winds may shift, the skies may change,
Yet side by side, we'll rearrange.
In unity, our spirits rise,
Together we glide, 'neath open skies.

With dreams in tow, we forge ahead,
Each step we take, full of what's said.
In this embrace, we forever bind,
Together we glide, hearts unconfined.

Signals in the Serenade

Whispers of the night arise,
Underneath the starlit skies.
Melodies of dreams express,
Echoes of the heart's progress.

Notes entwine like lovers' hearts,
Dancing where the silence starts.
Every chord a story told,
In the warmth, the night unfolds.

Strings of fate in twilight's glow,
Binding worlds we long to know.
Harmony in every sigh,
As the shadows softly fly.

In the breeze, soft tales will flow,
Crafted through the wayward glow.
Signals sent on moonlit waves,
Drawing out the songs we crave.

So let the serenade begin,
Whispering where dreams have been.
Each note a thread of light,
Guiding us through the night.

The Motion of Magic

In the twilight's gentle dance,
Spells are cast with every glance.
Whirling stars in velvet arms,
Enchanted by their silver charms.

Stars unite in cosmic flight,
Drawing dreams from depths of night
Every twirl, a secret shared,
Wonders of the heart laid bare.

A flicker here, a shimmer there,
Magic lingers in the air.
With each pulse, true wishes flow,
Lighting paths we long to know.

Moments woven, threads of fate,
In this dance, we hesitate.
But in this grace, we find our way,
Caught in time's unending play.

So sway to the rhythm's beat,
Feel the magic, so complete.
In every swirl, the world will show,
The dance of life, a wondrous glow.

Two to Tango Under the Stars

Beneath the dawn's soft embrace,
Two souls find their sacred space.
With each step, the night will sing,
In the dance, our spirits cling.

Hearts aligned in perfect time,
Every movement feels like rhyme.
Barefoot gliding on the ground,
In this love, we both are found.

Swirling colors paint the sky,
As we sway, we learn to fly.
In the shadows, dreams take flight,
Holding close through the moonlight.

Every spin, a story starts,
Binding tightly, two beating hearts.
With laughter woven into grace,
Lost in the magic we embrace.

Up above, the stars will twinkle,
As we dance, our spirits sprinkle.
Underneath this vast expanse,
Two to tango, lost in chance.

Cascades of Color

In the garden, colors bloom,
Painting life with sweet perfume.
Every petal, soft and bright,
Whispers with delight of light.

Turquoise skies and golden rays,
Dancing in the summer's blaze,
From deep violet to soft green,
Nature's palette, art unseen.

Brush of life, with strokes so bold,
Tales of joy and hearts of gold.
In the wind, the colors swirl,
Every hue begins to twirl.

Cascading down the gentle streams,
Reflections twist in woven dreams.
Color sings with every breeze,
Whispers sweet through swaying trees.

So let the hues paint all we see,
In the dance of harmony.
Life a canvas waiting there,
In these colors, we will share.

Partners in Motion

Two souls glide in gentle grace,
Beneath the stars, they find their place.
With every turn, they share a dream,
In whispered steps, their passions gleam.

Hands entwined, they move as one,
With laughter bright, until they're done.
The rhythm sparks their hearts to race,
In every leap, a warm embrace.

Through every twist, they feel the thrill,
Lost in wonder, time stands still.
With eyes that shine, they share the light,
Partners in motion, day and night.

In harmony, their spirits soar,
As love's sweet song, they both explore.
Each heartbeat echoes in the tune,
A dance that fades beneath the moon.

As shadows blend with evening's glow,
They revel in the passion's flow.
With every step, they dream once more,
Together bound, they seek the shore.

Unison on the Floor

Together they create a scene,
Where every clash becomes a dream.
With every sway, their bodies blend,
Unison rises, worlds extend.

In grace and rhythm, hearts align,
The beat of passion, pure, divine
In each embrace, they find their song,
A dance that feels forever strong.

With every whirl, they lose their place,
The music swells, a warm embrace.
In softest moments, magic grows,
A tapestry of love that glows.

In perfect time, they share the floor,
A bond so deep, forevermore.
Wrapped in silence, they take a chance,
Two souls entwined in timeless dance.

With every step, the world fades away,
As stars above begin to sway.
In unison, their hearts take flight,
Forever dancing into night.

Hearts that Sway

In twilight's glow, two hearts will sway,
Bound by love in soft display.
With every glance, a promise made,
A melody where dreams cascade.

Each gentle kiss ignites the spark,
In sync they move, lost in the dark.
With every touch, their spirits rise,
Two mystic souls beneath the skies.

In quiet moments, time slips by,
As whispered truths begin to fly.
In subtle steps, their passion grows,
A love that blossoms, ever glows.

Together they embrace the night,
Their laughter bright, a pure delight.
With whispered words, they feel the sway,
In tender heartbeats, love's ballet.

Through every trial, hand in hand,
They face the world, together stand.
In synchronized, sweet harmony,
Their hearts will sway eternally.

Choreographed Moments

In choreography of life, they dance,
Moving together, lost in chance.
With every step, a story unfolds,
Their journey marked by dreams and gold.

The stage is set, the music swells,
In harmony, their passion tells,
With each transition, they find their space,
Choreographed moments, filled with grace.

In laughter shared, the world seems bright,
As shadows play with flares of light.
Through every twist, they feel reborn,
In moments treasured, never worn.

With every heartbeat, they recreate,
An artful dance that won't abate.
In perfect sync, their souls entwine,
A testament to love's design.

As final bows draw near the close,
They'll remember how the passion flows.
In every step, a love unique,
Choreographed moments, hearts that speak.

Tangled in Time

Through corridors of dreams we roam,
Moments stitched like threads of chrome.
Whispers echo where shadows play,
Fleeting seconds drift away.

Amidst the tic-toc's gentle sigh,
Memories dance and often cry.
A tapestry where love entwines,
In the fabric of forgotten signs.

Lost in the labyrinth we create,
Every choice, a twist of fate.
Glimmers of hope in every turn,
In the silence, we discern.

Yet time's river flows unbound,
In its current, we are found.
Each heartbeat marks the space we fill,
In moments, our spirits thrill.

So let us wander hand in hand,
In this dance, forever planned.
Tangled threads of love will bind,
In the clock's embrace, we find.

The Art of Together

Two hearts painted in vibrant hues,
A canvas mingling varied views.
Brushstrokes gentle, firm, and free,
Creating tales of you and me.

In laughter's echo, colors blend,
In whispered secrets, hearts transcend.
A masterpiece of joy and tears,
Crafted through our fleeting years.

With every challenge, lines we trace,
A dance of love in time and space.
The art of life, we share and mold,
In every story, love is told.

Moments caught in a fraying net,
The shades of longing, no regret.
Together we'll compose and write,
A symphony of pure delight.

So hand in hand, we start anew,
In every shade of our deep blue.
The art of together, bold and bright,
In unity, we find our light.

Cadence of Memories

A rhythm flows through distant days,
In melodies of ancient bays.
Each note a fragment of who we are,
A song that echoes from afar.

In twilight's hush, our laughter rings,
Awakening the joy life brings.
Footsteps mark the paths we trace,
In every heartbeat, a sacred space.

Threads of sorrow, woven tight,
In shadows cast by fading light.
Yet every drop of rain that falls,
Brings forth wisdom, as it calls.

Echo chambers where memories stay,
In gentle whispers, they replay.
A cadence soft, a rhythm true,
Connecting me, connecting you.

So let us dance to this sweet song,
In every heartbeat, we belong.
With each soft cadence, we will climb,
Together through the stretch of time.

Pulses in the Dark

In shadows deep, a heartbeat flows,
Whispers of the night, nobody knows.
Flickering lights like fireflies,
Guiding dreams in velvet skies.

A pulse of longing in every sigh,
Silent wishes that seek to fly.
Underneath the blanket of night,
Hope ignites like stars so bright.

When shadows dance, the world feels small,
Yet in this dark, we hear the call.
With every thump, our fears unwind,
In the night's embrace, we find.

Though darkness lurks, our spirits rise,
With every heartbeat, truth defies.
In the depth where silence thunders,
We build our dreams in endless wonders.

So listen close to the pulse within,
A symphony where fears grow thin.
In the dark, we find our light,
A rhythm steady, bold and bright.

Echoes of Laughter

In the garden, children play,
Laughter dances in the air,
Sunlight glimmers on the sway,
Joyful moments, bright and rare.

Footsteps echo, hearts are light,
Chasing dreams beneath the sky,
In the warmth of day's delight,
Time, it whispers gently by.

Songs of joy, the breeze carries,
Tickling leaves, a soft embrace,
Every heartbeat, spirit varies,
Memories weave in time and space.

With each giggle, shadows fade,
Life unfolds in vibrant hues,
In this laughter, dreams are made,
A mosaic of shared views.

Evening falls, the stars appear,
Echoes linger, softly swell,
In our hearts, we hold it dear,
The laughter's timeless spell.

A Duet of Light

Morning breaks, the world awakes,
Sunbeams dance on golden streams,
Nature sings, the stillness quakes,
In harmony, the light redeems.

Two shadows stretch, a gentle sway,
Hearts aligned with every breath,
Through the dawn, we find our way,
In this union, life feels blessed.

Soft whispers in the softest glow,
Connection shines in twilight's grace,
In the silence, love will grow,
The universe, a warm embrace.

Hand in hand, the moments blend,
In the twilight, shadows merge,
Eternal love, our sweetest friend,
Together, we both surge.

As the stars begin to chime,
Side by side, we light the night,
In this duet, our lives entwine,
A symphony of pure delight.

Spirals of Joy

Round and round the colors spin,
In patterns wild, the heart takes flight,
Every turn a joyful grin,
Life's sweet dance in purest light.

In a circle, we laugh and twirl,
Each movement brings a spark anew,
Joy envelops, like a pearl,
In the moments, always true.

Let the winds of fortune blow,
Ride the waves of blissful sound,
In our hearts, the joy will grow,
On this journey, love unbound.

With every print, the world expands,
Painted dreams in vibrant hues,
Together we will make our plans,
In this dance, the love imbues.

As the evening softly glows,
We embrace the stars above,
In spirals of joy, the beauty shows,
Life's sweet song of endless love.

Embracing the Beat

Rhythms rise beneath the night,
Feet collide and hearts align,
In the music, pure delight,
Every pulse a sacred sign.

Hands wave high to chase the sound,
In this moment, free and bold,
Every beat, a love profound,
Stories shared, a joy retold.

Whispers echo through the crowd,
Voices lift with vibrant cheer,
Hearts enthralled, alive and loud,
Chasing dreams, we have no fear.

In the rhythm, souls entwined,
Every heartbeat, threads of grace,
In this dance, our spirits find,
Boundless hope in every space.

As dawn breaks, we hold the night,
Memories woven in the heat,
In the silence, pure delight,
Forever, we embrace the beat.

A Pirouette of Trust

In the dance of souls we twirl,
Every spin a secret unfurled.
A leap of faith, an open heart,
In each embrace, we find our part.

With every step we dare to share,
The weight of dreams hangs in the air.
In shadows cast, our fears confront,
Together strong, we bravely front.

Like whispers soft, our movements sway,
Binding us close, come what may.
A silent vow as we align,
In trust, dear friend, your hand in mine.

Through every rise, a fall to claim,
In every twist, we find our name.
Let go of doubt, let joy ignite,
Our pirouette shines through the night.

Spinning in Synchronicity

Two bodies weave a tale so bright,
In every spin, we find our light.
Matching rhythms, hearts entwined,
In this dance, our dreams aligned.

With every turn, we're swept away,
In harmony, we choose to play.
A mirrored glide, a seamless flow,
Through twists of fate, our passions grow.

The music plays, our spirits lift,
Each note a bond, a precious gift.
In perfect time, we dance as one,
Celebrating life, laughter spun.

Through ups and downs, we hold the line,
In synchronicity, hearts combine.
Together we'll chase the endless skies,
In this sweet dance where love never lies.

Echoes of Laughter

In the quiet hush of twilight's glow,
Giggles echo, soft and low.
With every smile, a story told,
Memories of joy, pure as gold.

Beneath the stars, we find our place,
In every jest, a warm embrace.
With every chuckle, spirits soar,
In laughter's arms, we long for more.

The rhythm of joy, so sweet, sincere,
In shared delight, our minds are clear.
Every moment, a chance to glide,
Through life's dance, we'll laugh, we'll ride.

In echoes rich, our bond extends,
Through laughter's charm, our hearts make amends.
With playful hearts, we leap and spin,
Echoes of laughter, where we begin.

The Language of Movement

In every grace, a word unspoken,
In every leap, our silence broken.
We touch the air with soulful art,
In fluid lines, we play our part.

Through gestures soft, we build a bridge,
With every sway, we cross the ridge.
A dance of faith, in sync we find,
The language of movement, so entwined.

In rhythms bound, our bodies learn,
The tales of past, the worlds we yearn.
With every twist, we shape our feel,
In every beat, our hearts reveal.

This silent song, a bond so pure,
In turning worlds, we'll always endure.
With every step, the story flows,
The language of movement forever grows.

The Poetry of Our Feet

We wander on paths both new and old,
Trails whisper stories waiting to be told.
Each step a word, each turn a rhyme,
In the dance of life, we bide our time.

Footprints in sand, on mountains so tall,
Echoes of laughter, a silken sprawl.
With every stride, we write our song,
In the journey, we find where we belong.

Barefoot on grass, in cities we roam,
Each corner we turn, we bring our home.
The poetry flows from soles worn thin,
In the language of motion, our hearts begin.

Through valleys and peaks, we embrace the street,
Life's rhythm resounds in the poetry of feet.
Together we wander, forever we'll see,
The stories we write, just you and me.

Colliding Dreams

In shadows of night, where whispers collide,
Dreams intertwine, fate won't hide.
Two souls reach out, like stars in a maze,
In the dance of desire, we set hearts ablaze.

Moments suspended, time drips slow,
Fleeting and fragile, like dew on a rose.
Reaching for visions, elusive yet true,
In the canvas of night, I find a part of you.

Voices like echoes, soft in the mist,
With every heartbeat, a tender tryst.
Building our worlds with each tender glance,
Lost in the opulence of tragic romance.

Defying the stars, we forge a new fate,
With each crashing wave, a love we create.
In the depths of our fears, together we stand,
As colliding dreams continue to expand.

Into the Pulse

In the heartbeat of cities, life starts to hum,
Rhythms of chaos, as hearts slowly come.
Each throb of emotion, a step into time,
We dance in the night, to fate's perfect rhyme.

Lights flicker like dreams, alive in the dark,
They pulse with a promise, ignite that spark.
Through alleys we wander, hand in hand tight,
Within the pulse, we are woven in light.

Moments like raindrops, they're fleeting and fast,
Yet treasures within them, forever will last.
Each whisper, each sigh, under moon's gentle gaze,
Into the pulse, we surrender in praise.

In symphonic splendor, our spirits ascend,
Lost in the music, we feel it blend.
To the rhythm of hope, our hearts make the beat,
In the pulse of the night, we find our retreat.

Serenade Under Stars

Beneath the vast tapestry of night,
Stars weave their magic, a delicate sight.
With voices so soft, we sing to the sky,
In this serenade, our spirits can fly.

The moon paints our dreams in silver and gold,
Whispers of secrets, in silence enfold.
With every soft note, the night sways and breathes,
In the embrace of darkness, love weaves and weaves.

Crickets join in with a symphonic tune,
While shadows invite the glow of the moon.
We dance under constellations so bright,
In this serenade, all worries take flight.

In moments like these, where two hearts align,
The universe hums, as your hand brushes mine.
Serenading the stars, we cherish the night,
With love as our savior, a beautiful plight.

Two as One in the Spotlight

Under the bright shining lights,
Two hearts dance in delight,
With every step they take,
The world fades from sight.

A rhythm that beats as one,
Their shadows twirl and spin,
A story of love begun,
In sync with the music within.

Laughter fills the air they share,
Together, they leap and sway,
In this moment, free from care,
They shine in a radiant display.

Each note a step closer near,
Binding them like a spell,
Through every whisper they hear,
In perfect harmony, they dwell.

When the curtain falls at night,
Two souls fade into one,
In the magic of their flight,
A dance that's just begun.

Harmony in Every Step

In the quiet of dawn's grace,
Two wander through the trees,
Every footfall finds its place,
Together swaying in the breeze.

Lively echoes of their dreams,
Like music on a stream,
In unison, they gleam,
Creating their own theme.

With laughter bright as the sun,
They chase the morning light,
Two souls, their journey begun,
Dancing with pure delight.

Through the fields of softest gold,
Hand in hand, they roam free,
Every secret they unfold,
In sweet harmony, they see.

As the day turns into night,
Stars illuminate their way,
With every step, love takes flight,
In their hearts, forever stay.

Embrace in Each Turn

In the dance of time's sweet flow,
Two figures twirl and spin,
Every turn a gentle glow,
With love that draws them in.

Eyes meet in a tender glance,
Whispers brush against their skin,
In every step, a chance,
To feel the warmth within.

With every spin, they're intertwined,
A bond that can't be broken,
In the music, they find,
The love that's ever spoken.

Through the shadows, they find light,
In each embrace, they soar,
With grace, they dance through the night,
Together, forever more.

When the final note is played,
Two souls in twilight's glow,
In the magic they've made,
Endless love starts to flow.

Synchronized Souls

In the stillness of the night,
Two hearts beat as one,
Guided by stars shining bright,
A journey just begun.

With every glance, a spark ignites,
Lighting paths unknown,
In the depth of shared delights,
Synchronized, they've grown.

Every laugh, a gentle chime,
Each sigh, a sweet embrace,
In this dance, lost in time,
Finding solace in their space.

As the world around them fades,
In each other, they confide,
Through the vibrant masquerades,
Their spirits open wide.

When dawn breaks with its light,
Hand in hand, they'll explore,
In the warmth of love's sight,
Synchronized forevermore.

Jointed Journeys

We walked on paths both old and new,
With every step, the world feels true.
The sky above paints dreams so bright,
And shadows dance in the fading light.

With laughter shared, our spirits soar,
Together we find what we're looking for.
Through twists and bends, our hearts will chart,
A tale of journeys, each a work of art.

Mountains high and valleys low,
In every challenge, our bond will grow.
Hand in hand, we face the tide,
In unity, we take this ride.

Echoes of joy in the winds that sing,
Moments cherished, the joy they bring.
With every turn, the future calls,
In this adventure, love never falls.

Ahead lies more than we can see,
An endless road, just you and me.
With hearts still open, dreams still bright,
We'll travel on, through day and night.

Moments in Motion

The clock ticks softly, time flows free,
Each instant captured, just you and me.
In a heartbeat's flash, the world can change,
Moments fleeting, yet feel so strange.

We laugh and dance, the music plays,
In this vibrant life, we lose our ways.
The rhythm of now, it pulls us near,
In every heartbeat, we conquer fear.

As sunlight fades and shadows creep,
We hold the memories, ours to keep.
In whispers shared beneath the stars,
We find our strength, no matter how far.

Each second lingers, each glance ignites,
In this grand tapestry, we find our sights.
Moments unravel, like threads so fine,
Together we weave, your heart with mine.

The present glimmers like dew on grass,
Where time stands still, and we let it pass.
With open arms and minds so bright,
We cherish each moment, day and night.

The Embrace of Time

Time wraps around us, gentle and kind,
Binding our stories, hearts intertwined.
In its embrace, we learn to grow,
Through tides of change, our spirits flow.

We dance through seasons, the years unfold,
In laughter shared, and tales retold.
Every heartbeat, a reminder sweet,
Moments of joy that our souls repeat.

As minutes flicker, like stars in the night,
We treasure the love that feels so right.
In twilight's glow, we find our peace,
In every hour, our woes release.

With time as a guide, we wander wide,
In every journey, you are my pride.
Together we savor what life imparts,
In the embrace of time, we share our hearts.

And when the dusk settles in with grace,
I'll hold your hand in this sacred space.
For in the arms of time's endless flight,
Our love will linger, a radiant light.

Patterns of Play

In fields of laughter, we run and spin,
Chasing the echoes of where we've been.
The world is painted in hues so bright,
As we create magic in every sight.

With playful hearts, we jump and shout,
In a dance of joy, there's never doubt.
Each game we play, a story told,
In patterns formed, our hearts unfold.

Through endless summers, our spirits rise,
In the simplest moments, we find our skies.
With every glance, we cast a spell,
In patterns of play, we know it well.

As seasons change and whispers fade,
The memories linger, the games we played.
In laughter's charm, we recognize,
The beauty found in youth'ssighs.

Forever dancing in life's ballet,
We cherish the patterns, the joy in play.
With open hearts and spirits kind,
In every moment, new joys we find.

Rhythms of Togetherness

In the pulse of our laughter, we dance,
Every heartbeat a step in the trance.
Hands joined tightly, we sway with delight,
In the rhythms of love, we shine ever bright.

Each note that we share, a sweet serenade,
In the warmth of this bond, we're never afraid.
Through storms and through sunshine, we're side by side,
With a symphony woven, our hearts as the guide.

In whispers of trust, our dreams intertwine,
Moments of joy like sweet vintage wine.
With grace in our moves, we write our own song,
In the dance of togetherness, we both belong.

Through laughter and tears, each chapter we weave,
In the tapestry formed, we learn to believe.
So let's share this journey, come what may,
In the rhythms of togetherness, we will stay.

Twirls Under Starlit Skies

Under the blanket of twinkling night,
We spin in circles, hearts feeling light.
With stars as our witness, we twirl and we sway,
In this magical moment, forever we'll stay.

The moon whispers softly, a gentle guide,
With every twirl, we feel the world glide.
Hand in hand, with dreams set aglow,
In the embrace of the night, love's rivers flow.

Our laughter like music, echoes so clear,
In the warmth of your presence, I hold dear.
With stardust around us, we lose all track,
In this dance of the night, there's no turning back.

With each playful spin, the universe gleams,
In the twirls under stars, we sweeten our dreams.
For in this soft moment, we're wild and free,
In the rhythm of twilight, just you and me.

Footsteps in Harmony

With every soft footfall, a melody plays,
In the dance of our lives, through the sun's golden rays.
Together we wander, paths intertwine,
In footsteps of harmony, our hearts align.

On the road less traveled, we sing our own tune,
In the warmth of the day or the glow of the moon.
With laughter as music, and love as our guide,
In footsteps of harmony, we stride side by side.

Through valleys and peaks, each moment we share,
In the silent communication, we truly care.
With every step forward, our stories unfold,
In the footprints of time, love's tale will be told.

Every stride marks a chapter, a memory dear,
In the dance of our journey, with you I have no fear.
So let's forge ahead, no matter the weather,
In footsteps of harmony, we're stronger together.

The Waltz of Friendship

In the grand hall of life, we waltz and we play,
With each gentle turn, we find our own way.
In the laughter we share, bonds grow ever strong,
In the waltz of friendship, together we belong.

Each spin tells a story, each step a new dream,
With trust as our partner, we flow like a stream.
In the rhythm of friendship, we'll never let go,
With hearts interlaced, in the softest glow.

Through seasons that change, we remain hand in hand,
In the dance of our journey, we both understand.
With joy as our guide, we'll face what is near,
In the waltz of friendship, there's nothing to fear.

So let's cherish these moments, embrace every chance,
In the warmth of each other, let's laugh and let's dance.
For in this sweet waltz, our spirits take flight,
In the bond of true friendship, everything feels right.

Whirling Through Life

In a dance of shadows and light,
We twirl in the grip of the night.
Moments cascade like leaves in the breeze,
Each heartbeat a whisper, a tease.

Through valleys of chaos, we glide,
Unraveling stories that time cannot hide.
With dreams as our sails, we chart the unknown,
Embracing the journey, never alone.

Life spins like a carousel bright,
Colors mingling, a beautiful sight.
In laughter and silence, we weave our own thread,
With every heartbeat, new paths are bred.

As seasons change, we find our way,
Through storms and sunshine, come what may.
In the whirling dance, we learn to be free,
Awash in the rhythm, just you and me.

A tapestry rich with hopes and fears,
Stitching together our smiles and tears.
We embrace the spin, the pull and the sway,
For in this crazy life, we long to stay.

A Shared Reverie

In the garden where dreams intertwine,
We linger in sunlight, your hand in mine.
Petals falling like soft spoken words,
In this moment, our hearts are birds.

We whisper secrets under the moon,
A melody played on a silvery tune.
With starlit eyes, we create a scene,
In this shared reverie, serene and keen.

Echoes of laughter dance all around,
In the quiet embrace, our souls unbound.
Images painted in twilight's glow,
Footprints of memories laid down below.

Waves of the night brush against our skin,
As we dream of the places we've never been.
With every heartbeat, a wish takes flight,
In the warmth of our shared delight.

Let the world slip away, just for a while,
Breath in the magic, share a smile.
In the softest whispers, our fears take flight,
Together we linger, lost in the night.

The Beat of Us

Underneath the starlit sky,
Our hearts drum a symphony high.
Each beat a promise, a shared refrain,
In the rhythm of love, we feel no pain.

Two souls entwined beneath the stars,
Echoes resonate, no distance too far.
With every pulse, the world is alive,
In harmony's warmth, we eagerly strive.

The cadence of laughter fills the air,
With every glance, an unspoken care.
In the chorus of dreams, we dance and sway,
As the beat of us guides the way.

We draw the map of our living song,
Finding the paths where we both belong.
A melody woven, soft and true,
In the rhythm of love, forever anew.

In unison, we march through the fight,
With hope as our lantern, we ignite the night.
In the beat of us, there's magic found,
Moving together, hearts light and unbound.

Interlaced Whispers

In the hush of twilight, we breathe as one,
Interlaced whispers, our journey begun.
Every secret shared, a thread gently spun,
In the fabric of time, our souls are undone.

Words flutter softly like leaves in the breeze,
Painting our moments with delicate ease.
With every sigh, we create a song,
In the magic of now, where we both belong.

Through labyrinths woven of dreams and desires,
Our voices entwined set the night afire.
Within the silence, our hearts lay bare,
Interlaced whispers, a promise to share.

As the stars bear witness, we find our way,
In the gentle glow of endearing play.
With laughter and love, we dance through the night,
Interlaced whispers, an unbreakable light.

Together we journey, through shadows and sun,
In this beautiful weave, our lives become one.
In the tapestry of time, forever we'll stay,
With interlaced whispers, come what may.

www.ingramcontent.com/pod-product-compliance
Ingram Content Group UK Ltd.
Pitfield, Milton Keynes, MK11 3LW, UK
UKHW021644200125
4187UKWH00003B/266